Spiders!

Intricate Masters of

zebra spider (Salticus scenicus)

Horror

Dr. Richard A. NeSmith

Love of Nature Series

ISSUE 28

Applied **P**rinciples of **E**ducation & Learning

APE-Learning *Publications*

© **2020 Richard A. NeSmith**
Love of Nature Series

dr.nesmith@gmail.com

https://amzn.to/3JVNlv7

MAY 2025

ISBN: 9798588737074

FLESCH-KINCAID GRADE LEVEL: 8.2

Spiders
(class Arachnida)

Most people are afraid of spiders! One of the most successful movies of 1990 was the comedy-horror film, *Arachnophobia,* grossing half a billion dollars. It has been estimated that 75% of the population is afraid of spiders. You might say *spiders give them the* **heebie-jeebies**! Or that spiders are intricate masters of horror! Granted, most people know very little about spiders, which may be why spiders are some of the most disliked animals on the planet. Sometimes fear is simply the *fear of the unknown.* We become anxious and distressed by what we do not understand. We are going to find that **spiders are really none of those things**.

For some of us, we don't mind spiders. I don't, except when they are caught on my hat and dangling in my face or

on the back of my neck. That motivates me to move quickly. This book should challenge the standing order that many people use on spiders, *squish first, and ask questions later.*

Spiny-backed orbweaver spider

Spiders are invertebrates belonging to the group of animals known as **Arachnids**. All spiders are arachnids, but not all arachnids are spiders. Arachnids also include mites, ticks, scorpions, and pseudoscorpions.[1] The spider's body is divided into the **cephalothorax** (the front part of the body covering the *head* and *thorax* region) and the **abdomen** (back stomach). Spiders are not insects but predaceous

arthropods[2] that are cunning and opportunistic **carnivores** (meat-eaters), hunters mostly eating insects.

They stalk, lie in wait, or pounce on prey. One species catches its prey as if slinging a slingshot with a spot of glue on the end of its silk thread. Another species slingshots itself rapidly toward its target.[3]

Range

Of the **60,000 species of Arachnids** found in habitats

---

[1] Scorpions and pseudoscorpions are arachnids but will not be addressed in this issue of *Love of Nature* due to space. Both of these will be addressed in a future issue. Pseudoscorpions are common, but rarely seen as they are so very small (1/16 to 1/8 inch long; 1.6-3.2 mm), tick-shaped critters with a large pair of pincers, but lacking the long tail and stinger of a true scorpion.

[2] Arthropoda is the largest group of land animals on the planet and also include crustaceans (crabs and shrimp), insects, and other animals with an exoskeleton and jointed legs. This means that arachnids are closely related to crabs.

[3] called slingshot spiders

worldwide, more than **45,000 are** known species of **spiders**. They live everywhere except in the North and South Poles, the air, and the oceans.[4] They are ranked at **#7** when it comes to *the most diversified living creatures in the world.* Of these, 3,000 species are present in North America. The most dangerous spiders on our continent are the **recluse**[5] and the **widow**[6] species. However, only an average of four people die from venomous spider bites a year in the United States.

In North America, most homes house three or four common spiders, often just called house spiders. On average, there are ***61.8 spiders found per home.*** Most spiders are so tiny in the home and nature that they are almost impossible to find, much less see. The general rule of thumb is that *"there is probably a spider within reach of you right now."* The global average spider density is approximately

Black widow spider

---

[4] Some spiders have inhabited freshwater lakes and ponds.
[5] Loxosceles
[6] Latrodectus

131 spiders per 116 square feet (10.8 square meters). That is just over one spider for every square foot. Some ecosystems have *twice* that number. Deserts and tundra, of course, are home to fewer spiders.

The spiders' unpopularity is undeserved because most spiders eat insects or other spiders, reducing pest populations. Very few spiders are health hazards. On the other hand, mites, ticks, and scorpions can cause serious health concerns. One harmless member of arachnids, however, is the daddy longlegs.

Characteristics

Though there are 11 diverse sets of arachnids, including three orders: Acari, Scorpiones, and Opiliones, they share some commonalities. Understanding these shared characteristics will be useful in understanding spiders, ticks, mites, and scorpions.

INTRODUCTION TO ARACHNIDS

Arachnids are a class of joint-legged invertebrates in the subphylum **Chelicerata** (meaning *claw horn*). They live mainly on land and are found in freshwater, and all aquatic environments, except for the open ocean. There are more than 100,000 named species. Some biologists believe there could be as many as 500,000 species not yet named or discovered.

There are eight characteristics that all Arachnids share. These include:

❶ **Eight legs (4 pair)**[7]

❷ **Two additional pairs of appendages: chelicerae** (for feeding and defense**); and pedipalps** (feeding, movement, and reproduction**).**

❸ The **body is organized into a fusion of the two parts: the head and thorax as one (called the cephalothorax), and the abdomen.**

❹ **Possess internal breathing systems: trachea, a book lung, or both.**

❺ **Mostly carnivorous, feeding on the pre-digested insect bodies of other small animals.**[8]

❻ **Most are venomous, releasing venom from special glands that kill or immobilize prey or predators.**

❼ **Some (mites) are parasitic, and some are carriers of diseases (ticks).**

❽ **Typically lay eggs, which hatch into immature arachnids similar to adults. Scorpions, however, give birth to live young.**

Spiders are *not* insects. But insects do make up the diet of most spiders. With all but two spiders being venomous, the purpose of spider venom is to paralyze their prey. Most spiders are too small to bite or affect humans, but there are a few whose bites can cause localized pain, just as can the

---

[7] This is the easiest means of identifying an arachnid. It also differentiates arachnids from insects, for all insect have six legs (3 pair). In addition, Arachnids do not do not have antennae or wings as do most insects.

[8] There are at least 95 species of arachnids (including mites and harvestmen) reported as eating plant matter (nectar, sap, or pollen).

sting of a bee or wasp.

Body Organization

Arachnids have eight legs (**appendages**), all attached to the cephalothorax. The first pair is used for feeding and are called **chelipeds** (pronounced *keel-a-peds*) or the

chelicerae. These are the spider's muscled jaws used to hold their prey while being injected. On the tip of the chelicerae are the **fangs** (long, pointed hollow teeth). These natural injection needles, make them well-suited for piercing the exoskeletons of prey.

Venom sacs contain the toxins, while **venom ducts** extend through the chelicerae or under the **carapace**. These ducts open near the tips of the fangs. Females have larger venom sacs than males. Some adult male spiders don't have functioning venom sacs at all. When a spider bites, the fangs move out of their furrow and pierce the prey. Simultaneously, venom is injected through a tiny opening at the tip of the fang.

The second pair of appendages are called **pedipalps** (or just palps). These have various uses, including just acting as a second pair of legs. Palps are sometimes modified as **pinchers** for protection or immobilizing prey. However, their primary function in males is to provide a way to transfer sperm to the female. The walking legs make up the remaining four pairs. Each leg ends in two or three very tiny claws, which aid in walking, grasping, and climbing on steep, uneven surfaces, such as walls. The middle claw is especially important for web spiders because they use it to catch hold of the silk threads of their webs.

The arachnid's body is encased in a tough, flexible, but fibrous and durable polysaccharide[9] called **chitin**. This material makes up the **exoskeleton** or **cuticle**. Some species have a thickened area on the cephalothorax's upper

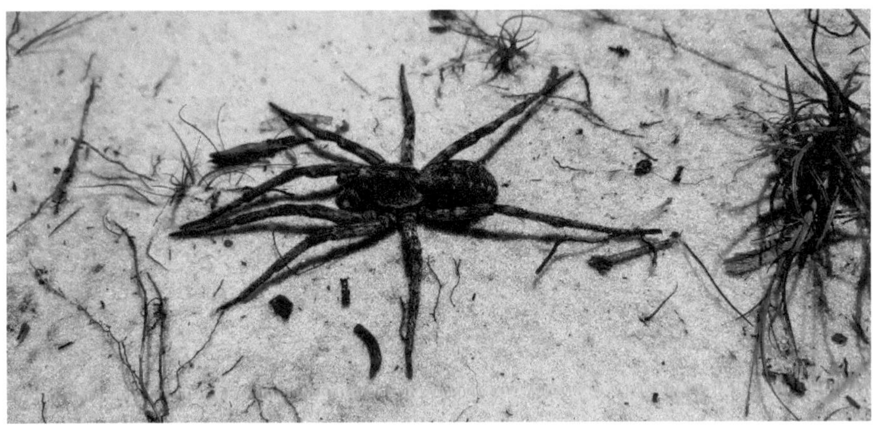

Author took this photo of a wolf spider one fall midnight using a bright floodlight. The light seem to not cause any alarm or anxiety for the spider though it sat still the entire time being observed.

back. This structure is called a **carapace** (protein-thickened tough covering).

It is hard and sturdy and protects the internal organs but being invertebrates, it also provides a means of attaching muscles and fibers. However, it restricts the spider from being able to grow.

Growth can only occur if the spider **molts**, a vulnerable period in which it will shed its old body.[10] This is done quite frequently throughout its juvenile time, though some adult spiders molt their entire life.

---

[9] glucose monomers

[10] The molting process can take up to two hours and leaves the spider virtually defenseless.

Respiration

These animals breathe oxygen and release carbon dioxide. However, arachnids do not have traditional lungs. Instead, they have specialized **organs** called **book lungs**, **trachea**, or both. The book lungs membranes are thin blood-filled tissues. The tracheae are pipes or tubes with **spiracles** that connect directly to the exoskeleton. Air travels through the spiracles, across the sensitive membranes, into the trachea or the book lungs. As the air circulates, **oxygen** is exchanged entering the bloodstream, and **carbon dioxide** (a waste gas) is removed, then

travels out the membranes through the spiracles.

Circulation

Arachnids have hearts and blood vessels that pump their blood (called **hemolymph**) to all parts of their body. However, the blood is not found in those vessels but is dumped into the body cavities. There it bathes all organs. Whereas mammals have iron in their blood, arachnids contain a copper content. This copper causes the spider or scorpion's blood to appear bluish.

Vision and Sensory Organs

Except for cave-dwelling spiders or scorpions, arachnids have eyes located at the front of the cephalothorax or along the sides. Many have four, six, or eight eyes. Other spiders have as many as 12 eyes. Most arachnids can detect only between light and dark, while others have a well-developed vision. There are two basic kinds of eyes called **ocelli**: the lateral (to the side) and the median (towards the center). The lateral ocelli are **compound eyes** and may have a **tapetum**, enhancing the ability to collect light.[11] Scorpions can have up to five lateral ocelli pairs, but there are never more than three pairs present for the others.

---

[11] Compound eyes are usually large. The larger compound eyes consist of thousands of ommatidia (plural). Each is composed of a group of photoreceptor cells surrounded by support cells and pigment cells. The outer part of the ommatidium (singular) is covered with a clear cornea, lens, and photoreceptor cells, identifying differences in brightness and color. The cornea is the transparent part that covers the front part of the eye. Its function is to refract (bend) light.

There is a **cornea** and a **retina** present. However, the retina probably does not have enough light-sensitive cells to allow the eyes to form a proper image. It would seem that the arachnids' vision is more of recognizing movement

and various levels of light instead of image formation. Their visual perception is only a relatively coarse image. So only objects close by can serve as visual stimuli. Such is apparent during mating rituals where the male waves the large chelipeds before the female to gain her attention.

Possibly more important than eyesight are **tactile sensors**. These fine sensory hairs cover the body and give the animal its sense of *touch*.[12]

Finally, another essential sensory is called **slit sense organs**. These are slit-like **pits** *covered* with a thin membrane. Inside the pit is a small hair that touches the underside of the membrane and detects **motion**. Slit sense

---

[12] Some of these tactile sensors are relatively simple, but some are complex structures called trichobothria.

organs[13] are believed to assist arachnids in the perception or awareness of their body's position and movement, and possibly also hearing.

Not only are the slit sense organs used for a form of hearing, but so are the legs. The vibration-sensing hairs on the spider's legs are sensitive to sensations and pressure, thus feeling and reporting, just like a human's ear. So, that time you ran into a spider web and screamed, that spider heard you. A recent study suggests that a spider can hear a surprising range of sounds from more than six feet away,

---

[13] Called proprioceptors.

thanks to these sensory organs on its legs.

These hairs also help arachnids detect **air currents**, which is vital in detecting captured prey and for orientating an orbed web. These senses enable the arachnids to catch prey, avoid **predators** and danger, and seek potential mates.

Social and Organized

While most spiders are **solitary** and even aggressive or hostile towards their own, some are **social**. Hundreds of species tend to live in groups called **colonies** that build

nests. Such cooperative communities have their advantages. Often a *communal web* is built in which multiple spiders work together to subdue their prey, usually larger than themselves. Colonies often grow big enough to capture large insects, as well as small birds and bats.

Another benefit of colony living is the cooperation in maintaining the nest and webs. This collaboration enables more silk production than a single individual could yield. Defending the nest or web also becomes teamwork, much like seen with social bees or wasps.

Silk Production

Spider silk primarily consists of proteins.[14] **Silk** is produced when glands secrete a liquid protein in the abdominal (or rear) part of spiders, called a **spinneret** because they *spin* the substance. When these gels combine and leave the duct, it turns into a solid fiber as it mixes with the air. As the mixture is sprayed, the silk becomes dry from the spider's

---

[14] that possess large quantities of nonpolar and hydrophobic amino acids like glycine or alanine.

abdomen, immediately upon combining with air, forming a thread.

The extraordinary mechanical and stretchable (**tensile**) strength[15] of spider silk has been compared to steel. It is estimated that spider silk is five to one hundred times stronger than steel (strength-to-density ratio).[16] It has also been suggested that if the web were human-sized, it would be tough enough to snag a jetliner. Besides its strength and stickiness, it also absorbs the energy of the struggling prey. The more the captured struggles, the more entangled they become.

Web building

Another way of identifying or classifying spiders is by their web design. Though not all webs are used to capture prey, most spiders can be identified by the type of web they spin.

---

[15] the resistance of a material to breaking under tension
[16] silk is much stronger for its size than a steel beam

Many spiders build new webs each night or day.

Some spiders are **orb weavers**, and most orbital webs are reconstructed twice a day. Spiders can build a new **orb web** in about one hour. An orb web is a sequence of wheel-shaped, circular outlines, with spokes extending from a center. Many species of spiders weave orb webs, which are beautiful and most noticeable in the morning dew. When the spiderweb is rebuilt, the spider will eat and redigest the silk to save (recycle) the resources. The orb web's efficiency

is found in its strategic placement and the breeze between the two trees or bushes used as anchors. A nicely placed web can catch up to 200 insects per day.

Tangle web spiders, also called cobweb spiders and comb-footed spiders, are recognized for building three-dimensional *space webs*. This is a large group of spiders with over 2,200 species. This includes the common house spider and the notorious black widow. These tangled webs spiders like to build in corners, attics, wood, and debris piles, in hollow stumps, and under stones. Tangle web spiders hang upside down in the middle of their webs, waiting for ants

or crickets to get tangled up. Many tangled web spiders trap ants and other ground-dwelling insects using elastic, sticky silk trap lines leading to the soil surface. Upon careful observation, one can usually see a small funnel opening near the top of the web. Female spiders produce egg sacs with 400 to 1,000 babies. Spiderlings have little chance as most are eaten before they mature.

Another form of a web is called a **sheet web**. These are usually constructed low to the ground between shrubs and trees and also between blades of grass. One spider that creates sheet webs is the **hammock spider**.[17] Their webs are flat and sheetlike and dome- or cup-shaped. The spider is usually found on the lower side of the web and often *between two layers* of webbing. The hammock spider, native to North America, builds a hammock-shaped web. The horizontal sheet webs (see photo above) are quite a sight after rain or early in the morning as they catch dew and

---

[17] Linyphia *phrygiana* and Linyphia *montana*

hold the water as unique droplets.

The *most common type of webs is the* **funnel webs**. There are over 300 species[18] of funnel weaver spiders, of which most are harmless to humans.[19] **Funnel webs** are found in wooded areas, small bushes, trees, and grass. Funnel weaver spiders are usually brownish or grayish, ranging from 1/3 to 2/3 inches (8.5-17 mm) when fully grown. They have four pairs of eyes roughly the same size. The legs and body are hairy, and the legs typically have dark banding. They are often mistaken for wolf spiders, but the scope and pattern of eyes can most easily distinguish them. Like wolf spiders, the funnel weavers are swift runners.

Diet

Arachnids are **predators** of insects and other invertebrates,

---

[18] Such as the large grass spider family Agelenidae.
[19] The Australian funnel web spider is considered one of the world's deadliest spiders.

and sometimes small fish and birds.[20] The exception is mites, which feed on all kinds of things, like fungi, plants, dead animals, and bacteria.

Arachnids do not have teeth, so they do not chew their

---

[20] Such as 1) semi-aquatic spiders catching and eating small freshwater fish such as mosquitofish and, 2) the South American goliath bird-eating spider.

food. As a result, arachnids only *eat* liquid food. In other words, they *drink* their meals. To do this, the carnivorous ones use **chelipeds** with **fangs**. With these, they inject digestive and potent **neurotoxins**[21] into their prey.[22] The neurotoxins disable their catch, and the digestive

chemicals[23] break down the prey's tissues, liquefying the insides. Ingestion is simply a matter of sucking or pumping out the liquid soup.

Since more than 80 percent of the spiders are predatory, they utilize silk to capture, trap, or immobilize prey. Some free-hunting species directly attack but may wrap the caught creature in silk afterward. Others build web traps.

---

[21] These neurotoxins exert toxic effects in the vertebrate central nervous system by depolarizing neurons, and increasing uncontrolled exocytosis of neurotransmitters from nerve terminals.
[22] Both secretions contain an array of active proteins.
[23] In essence, an arachnid digests its food outside of its own stomach.

Habitats

Some spiders can tolerate temperatures as cold as 23 degrees Fahrenheit (-5 degrees C)— well below freezing. These spiders produce **glycerol**, similar to automobile

antifreeze. However, the process is slow and requires time for spiders to build up enough glycerol to survive such cold temperatures. Spiders, and insects in general, can tolerate temperatures up to about 110°F (43.3°C) before it becomes lethal. Temperature restrictions are more about proteins, particularly enzymes, malfunctioning if and when these go above or below their functional temperature range. Outside those parameters the enzymes fail to function properly, thus the cause of loss of life.

Apart from such physiological ranges, spiders, like insects and other invertebrates, can and will survive if there is an available food and water source, housing, and a feasible environment for reproduction. Some spiders do not even live on land but instead on the water (such as fishing spiders) or underwater (diving bell spiders). And a few arachnids live as parasites on the webs of other spiders.

Reproduction

Arachnids reproduce sexually, meaning that they require combining **gametes** (male sperm and female eggs) from both sexes. In the case of arachnids, however, the male's **sperm** is not inserted into the female's body from within the male's genitals. Instead, courtship is successful when the male injects his sperm (encased in a bulb) from his **pedipalps**[24] into the female's genital opening (**epigyne**), found on the underside of the female's abdomen.

With spiderlings in tow.

Spiders can lay a large number of eggs very quickly. Depending on the species, some will lay between two and 1000 eggs. As the eggs are laid, the female spider will wrap them in a silken **egg sac**, which is then hidden in a web or carried with the female while foraging. Female brown and black widows, for example, can produce 10 to 20 egg sacs in their lifetime, each containing between 150 to 300 eggs.

---

[24] (or palps, the second pair of leg-like appendages)

Spider eggs can typically hatch in two to three weeks, depending on the species or the season.

Arachnid females lay yolky eggs, which hatch into immatures that resemble adults (**spiderlings**). However,

scorpions are either **ovoviviparous** (through eggs that are hatched within the parent's body) or **viviparous** (live young that have developed inside the parent's body), depending on species, bearing live young.

Some arachnids carry their eggs or their newly hatched offspring on their back for a period of time. As spiderlings hatch, they usually settle close to the nesting area for several weeks before moving on and staking out their own territory, which sometimes might involve a relatively long flight. For some spider species, the mother dies after she lays her eggs.

Arachnids have so many offspring! Without wings, **dispersal** could become an issue as the offspring could become competitors with their parents or siblings. Or worse, begin to eat each other. However, dispersion does occur but is passive and occurs in several ways. One way arachnids do this is by **ballooning** (also called kiting).

Using strands of silk, young spiders can move from place to place airborne with the air currents.[25] Some mites disperse passively by using threads of silk or using their own bodies as a carrying surface, which acts like a parachute *caught* in the wind.

Sometimes dispersal is in **clumps**, especially if the offspring are of a social colony-forming species. Other times, a lack of food or resources might cause a more random dispersal of the young. By utilizing some of the sensors already mentioned, young arachnids will cast a long, lightweight silk thread[26] into the wind and be

---

[25] There is also a phenomenom here with the electric current-charged atmosphere. Ballooning spiders operate within this planetary electric field. When their silk leaves their bodies, it typically picks up a negative charge. This repels the similar negative charges on the surfaces on which the spiders sit, creating enough force to lift them into the air. See: http://bit.ly/3oexeLP

[26] This thread is called a gossamer thread which is very light and thin. It is a delicate, transparent cobweb seen on grass or bushes or floating in the air in calm weather, especially during autumn.

taken up into the sky. Some have been found floating around at 30,000 feet (900,144 meters).

The average lifespan of a spider is one to two years but up to eight years. However, the lifespan of a "house spider" depends on the region one lives. Different spiders are native to other places, and the length of their lifespan depends on the species.

Common Types of North American Arachnids

Some of the most common house spiders, mites, and ticks are noted below to help us become better acquainted.

1. AMERICAN HOUSE SPIDER[27] is common in most of North America and is the most commonly encountered

One of the American common house spider species.

spider in the United States. It is a comb-footed spider with long, skinny legs with comb-like hairs. As adults, their size is between 0.2 to 0.35 inches (4-9 mm). Males tend to be smaller than females. They are usually yellowish-brown with a dullish white, extended abdomen with spots. Males tend to be darker and smaller than females.

---

[27] Genus/species: Parasteatoda *tepidariorum*

This spider typically lives near humans, such as in closets, high corners, window frame angles, under furniture, garages, sheds, barns, basements, and crawlspaces. They prefer dark and dry environments and generally feed on flies, mosquitoes, ants, beetles, cockroaches, and wasps. They are not aggressive towards humans unless they are threatened, challenged, grabbed, or squeezed. This spider's bite can be painful but not lethal to humans, unlike their cousins, the Black Widow spider. Some bites are *dry*, meaning that *no venom is injected* and the victim has no response (and may not even know they were bitten).

When the spider's meal is finished, it will cut loose the dry, drained insect shell and let it fall to the ground below the web without rebuilding the web. Close observation of the ground under an established spiderweb can often reveal the spider's diet.[28]

2. WOLF SPIDER[29] is common throughout the U.S. but is particularly prevalent in Texas, California, and Missouri. They are hairy, quick, and relatively large, and spiders are sometimes mistaken for tarantulas[30] or brown recluse spiders. They are vigorous and agile independent hunters with excellent eyesight, live mostly in solitude, and do not spin webs. They are drifters that lie in ambush. Wolf spiders depend on **camouflage** and are usually gray, black, and brown.

Hogna carolinensis, commonly known as the Carolina wolf spider, is found across North America. It is the largest wolf

---

[28] if the husk has not already been harvested by other insects
[29] Family Lycosidae
[30] Tarantulas are important desert spiders and will be address in a future *Love of Nature* issuef.

spider on the continent, typically measuring 0.7-0.8 inches (18–20 mm) for males and 0.75 to 1.3 inches (22–35 mm) for females.

These spiders are usually found on the ground and under rocks and debris. They live in various habitats, such as forests, fields, gardens, graveled riverbanks, and rocky beaches. Wolf spiders do not build webs as they prefer to live in burrows. They usually enter homes, especially during autumn when seeking warmth, by way of windows, doors, garages, basements, and house plants. Wolf spiders often jump on their prey, hold it between their legs, and roll over on their backs, trapping their prey with their limbs before biting it.

Black widow spider

Wolf spiders are not aggressive towards people, and some have even made these pets. They generally do not attack humans unless threatened. Bites are moderately painful and cause redness and itchiness but lessen quickly. Biting is a last resort, and before biting, they generally will retreat or rear up on their back legs, revealing their large fangs. They can be scary as they scurry under doorways or jump on one's clothing or across one's lap.

3. BLACK WIDOW SPIDER[31] females are shiny black with red, orange, or yellow spots or an hourglass shape on their abdomen's underside. This spider is one of the few species harmful to people in North America. Black widows often feature a red hourglass shape on their underbelly side. The black widow is notoriously considered the most venomous spider in North America. Its bite, however, is rarely fatal to humans.

Their comb-like foot can also be recognized, as a row of firm, curled hairs on the hind pair of legs. The males don't

Black widow spider withred hourglass markings on bely.

have the red pattern and are half the size of the females.

---

[31] Western black widow (Latrodectus *hesperus*) and Southern black widow (Latrodectus *mactans*).

They prefer building their webs near the ground in dry and dark locations, the underside of ledges, on plants, in cracks of or under rocks, debris, outdoor furniture, railings, woodpiles, or stone walls. They're very **solitary** spiders, only socializing during the mating time for **copulation**. Typically, the black widow spider will eat the smaller male spider after receiving the male's sperm.[32] However, this is *true of most spider species.*

The wound from the bite will look like one or two fang marks, with small red-like spots. And though the bite itself is not particularly painful, it may even go unnoticed. Pain follows 10–60 minutes afterward in the lymph node

regions. From here, it spreads to the muscles, and muscle cramps develop. One's abdominal muscles become very rigid. Symptoms include chills, fever, nausea or vomiting, sweating, severe belly or back pain, headache, high blood pressure, stupor, restlessness, and shock. If bitten, immediate medical attention should be sought. It is

---

[32] It has even been observed that should a female black widow stop eating the male, that the male will seek to put himself back in her jaws! Talk about dedication and a mission!

believed that the toxin can pass the blood-brain barrier, thus directly attacking the central nervous system.

4. BROWN RECLUSE SPIDER is widespread in North America, especially *abundant* in the south-central Midwest from southeastern California through New Mexico and

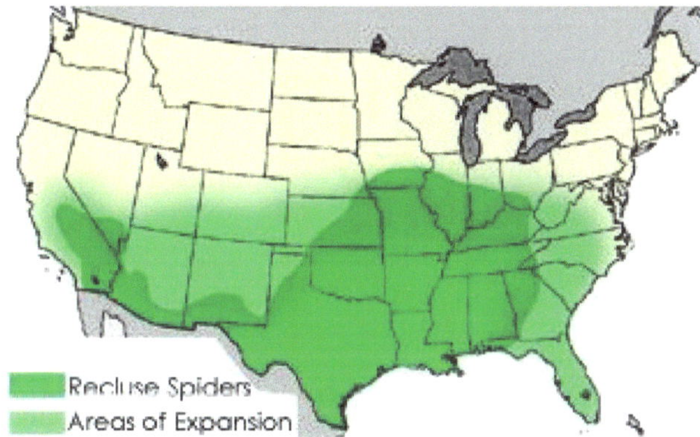

Arizona's southern borders. They are found in nearly all of Texas and Nebraska's southeast corner across into southern Ohio, then south to Georgia and the Gulf Coast states (see map). These spiders live in homes unaware of the homeowners but seldom seen. Though the spiders do not travel around, they can be transported in luggage or freight, but it is uncommon to find a brown recluse outside its native range. Those that do often do not survive or mate.

The violin-shaped markings on their back best identify it. These patterns lead to their commonly being referred to as *fiddleback* or *violin spiders*. With only six eyes arranged in pairs in a semicircle, they look different than the spiders with the regular eight ocelli. They grow from ¼ to ½ inches (6-11 mm) are light to dark brown with a solid-colored abdomen covered in fine hairs.

Their name originates from their shyness, being nocturnal and generally avoiding humans. They build their webs in dark, secluded places as in a crawlspace or deep in the back of a closet. They often are transported in furniture boxes from infested locations. One female can produce 150 or more spiderlings a year.

They rarely bite unless provoked, such as getting caught in bed linen or clothing. Like the black widow, bites can go unnoticed for a few hours before the severity of the symptoms set in. Often a small white blister will appear and then become hardened. **Necrosis** (*dying* tissue) can occur, and **gangrene**[33] can set in unless treated, creating an open wound.

5. DADDY LONGLEGS (Opiliones) are technically not *spiders* and are called harvestmen, harvest spiders, or shepherd's spiders.[34] These are harmless with long, thin legs and bodies fused, giving the appearance of one long oval figure. They are gray to brown with some banding markings. Harvestmen have no silk glands, so they do not build webs but lurk in the dark and damp corners. They eat small insects like mosquitoes and flies. So they can be quite effective at pest control. Opiliones

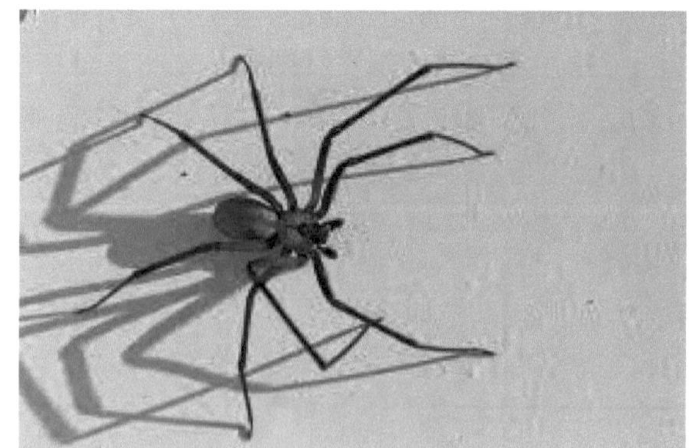

---

[33] Gangrene is a diagnosis of an infection caused by Clostridium *perfringens*, in which the blood becomes contaminatede causing tissue to die and turn dark and hard.

[34] Only one of them is a spider. Opiliones are a distinct order that is not closely related to spiders. They can be easily distinguished from long-legged spiders by their fused body regions and single pair of eyes in the middle of the cephalothorax. See: https://www.lexico.com/explore/is-a-daddy-long-legs-a-spider

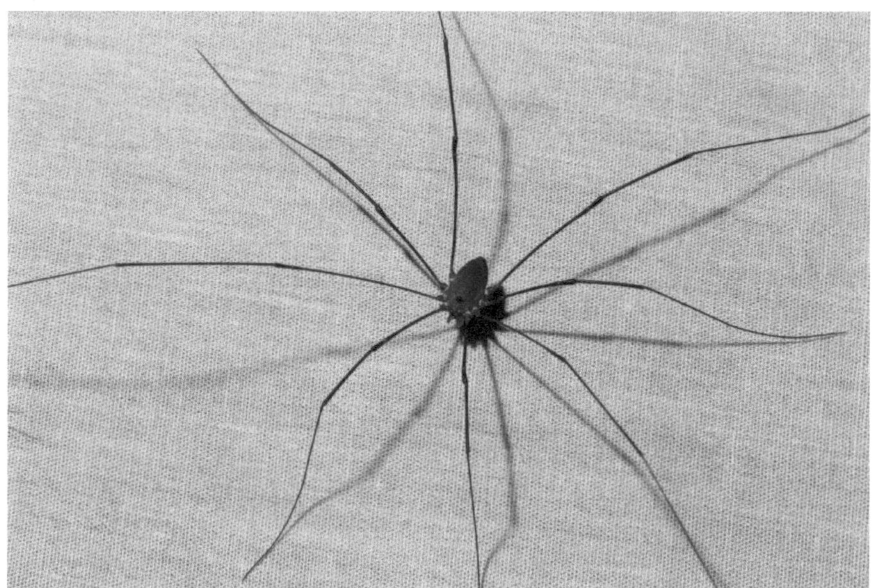

in North America are spiders, so they do possess venom sacs except for one species (which consumes only plants). Their venom is very mild and virtually non-toxic to humans. Their fangs are too small or weak to bite or have much effect on humans.

6. JUMPING SPIDER[35] is common in North America with over 5,000 species and is easily identified by their relatively large size and shimmering chelicerae (see photo page 40). They tend to be medium-sized spiders that hop or jump onto their prey, sometimes leaping up to 25 times their own body length.

Jumping spiders are **diurnal** and abundant in grassland and prairie environments, but most states have a few species. Their webs are more like *pup tents* that protect eggs and are often found in yards or barns. Jumping spiders are some of the fastest-moving arthropods on Earth and are famous for

---

[35] Phidippus *audax*

their agility.

7. SOUTHERN HOUSE SPIDER (see photo page 41)

males and females, though covered in very fine hair, but look entirely different from one another (**sexual dimorphism**). Males are larger, amber-brown, and longer legs. In contrast, the females are charcoal gray with large rounded bulging bodies. Females are sometimes mistaken for **tarantulas** and males for brown recluse spiders.

The Southern House spider is most common in the Southern United States and along the Southern West Coast. These house spiders prefer living in people's homes. They are often found in the dark recesses of window sills, shutters, overhangs, and other dim places in the home. They particularly enjoy building webs in yucca plants.

Females are rarely seen and seldom move except to capture prey caught in their webs. House spiders have a lifespan of up to eight years. Males are more active, appear more aggressive, and will search for prey, but have a shorter lifespan. Their mouthparts are too small to penetrate human flesh. Being nearly blind, they tend to scare people, for they have a habit of crawling across anything in their

Giant house spider (Tegenaria *gigantea*)

path.

8. ORB-WEAVER SPIDER *(Araneidae)* rarely bite and only do so when threatened and unable to escape. If bitten by an orb weaver, the bite and injected venom are comparable to a bee sting, with no long-term implications unless the victim is **hyper-allergic** to the venom.

Orb weavers can be very small or relatively large, depending on the species and the age. As orb-weavers age, they are inclined to produce less silk, so many adult orb-weavers rely more on their coloring to attract more prey. The most remarkable web design belongs to the orb weavers. Those of the common garden spider indeed represents the best-known and most recognized type of all webs. As insects mistakenly fly into a web, they become

stuck to the sticky threads. The spider quickly moves to immobilize from the web's hub to bite or wrap its victim.

Miscellaneous

Though they have not been discussed in detail, **ticks**, **mites**, and **scorpions** are also very important arachnids in the ecosystem. To do them justice, they will be addressed in

their own future issue of the *Love of Nature.*

Spiders rest, but they do not sleep in the same way that humans do. Instead, they do have daily cycles of activity and rest like us. Spiders do not have eyelids so they cannot close their eyes. Still, they reduce their activity levels and lower their metabolic rate to conserve energy. Hunting spiders are much more active. Many of them are **nocturnal** predators and spend the day hidden away in a nest or under a rock to conserve energy and avoid fellow predators.

Spider infestations can be avoided by reducing clutter in

unused areas of the home. This minimizes possible hiding places. If spiderwebs are visible, use caution before approaching the area. If a black widow or brown recluse spiders are suspected, seek the help of an exterminator. In addition, prevent entry points like cracks and poorly screened windows or doors.

Spiders are scary. Well, spiders *can be* scary. Spiders are just another relatively safe and neutral animal living in the various ecosystems to which they have adapted. They serve an **ecological niche**. Without them, there would be numerous issues, some we cannot even imagine. **Spiders! Heebie-Jeebies?** No, and they are not even intricate masters of horror. If you learn about them, they are just

another essential animal in the **intricate** Jenga puzzle of nature. To know them is to respect them. But you do not need to fear them anymore.

REVIEW

1. Where can spiders be found?

2. How many different spider species are found in North America?

3. What are the chances of dying from a spider bite?

4. How many legs do a spider have, and where are they connected to its body?

5. Too many spiderlings nearby could cause parents to compete with their offspring. How is this generally avoided?

6. Why can't spiders simply bite and chew their food?

7. What are the two main products found in a spider's venom?

8. If you were to fall into a spider-infested pit accidentally, what kind of spider would you hope these to be?

9. What two spiders are considered the most dangerous in North America?

10. From reading this book, what things did you find that nearly all spiders have in common?

ORB-WEAVER SPIDER

COLORING PAGE

http://www.supercoloring.com/coloring-pages/spider-on-its-web

Name:________________________

Spiders! Intricate Masters of Horror

Carefully read each statement or clue. Record the answer in the appropriate boxes. Use the Word Bank if needed.

appendages   cephalothorax   motion   ocelli   spinneret   eight   toxins   Arachnida   carnivore   health

Chelicerata   blue   chitin   trachea   chelipeds   diversified

Across

3. Four, six, eight, or maybe even twelve?
4. Venom sacs contain the ________.
8. Means 'claw horn.'
12. The spiders body is divided into the ______ and the abdomen.
14. How many legs does a spider have?
15. First pair is used for feeding or to hold prey

Down

1. Gland that secretes silk.
2. Purpose of the slit sense organs is to detect ______.
4. Used by spiders to breathe?
5. Spiders are the most ________ living creatures in the world.
6. Eat meat!
7. What taxonomic class are spiders from?
9. Another word for legs?
10. Substance making up the exoskeleton.
11. Color of the hemolymph
13. Very few spiders are _________ hazards.

INTERESTING SOURCES TO CONSIDER

Biggest Orb Weaver Spider: Are they Dangerous? Awesome Animals. Available at: https://youtu.be/JW7tLXeIv3M

Facts About Spiders: Secret Nature. Spider Documentary. Natural History Channel. Available at: https://youtu.be/kY7ylZ_5B7w

Is A Daddy-long-legs A Spider? Available at: https://www.lexico.com/explore/is-a-daddy-long-legs-a-spider

MonsterQuest: Monster Spiders (S2, E17). Full Episode. Available at: https://youtu.be/d3RureH3Eso

National Geographic Super Spider Documentary. Available at: https://youtu.be/oR-XltI_VMg

North American Spider Identification Available at: https://youtu.be/NH1Cm9IFQPQ

Spiders: The Whole Story S01E02 - The Secrets of Nature. Available at: https://youtu.be/NdQB2QNsMfw

The Most Aggressive Spiders in the World. Available at: https://youtu.be/u6VW3aR6FQY

The Weird World Of Spiders: Wild About S1 EP6. Real Wild. Available at: https://youtu.be/rXDvzgkFXnY

Ultimate Guide to Spiders. Available at: https://youtu.be/EJEH6MhNiPI

Wasp Spider Documentary: Planet Doc Express. Available at: https://youtu.be/emeiTvMnT4A

Webs of Intrigue [Full Documentary]. Available at: https://youtu.be/ZSM44UxwtSw

Wild The Spider Hunter World' 's Deadliest Animals. Documentary National Geographic. Available at: https://youtu.be/mYSwpuPZQQM

ABOUT THE AUTHOR

Richard NeSmith is a native of Florida, USA. He grew up wading through the swamps of central Florida with his two younger brothers during the pre-Disney era and unknowingly, falling in love with biology, wildlife, and nature. He has lived in seven American states, twice in Australia, and once in Mexico City. He holds eight university degrees and has taught for 14 years in secondary schools, here and abroad, and another 13 years as a professor in several American universities. His service includes professor of science education, Dean of Education, Campus Dean, as well as an online instructor. His passion for learning (and *how we learn*) did not develop until *after* graduating from high school. His only explanation for this is that *having a goal made all the difference in the world*. He enjoys reading, hiking, nature photography, golf, tennis, R.V. camping, and travel.

http://richardnesmith.obior.cc

Applied **P**rinciples of **E**ducation & Learning *presents*

APE-Learning

AMAZON AUTHOR's PAGE:

https://www.amazon.com/author/richardnesmith

Educational, wildlife, and naturalist books
Dr. Richard NeSmith.

Issue 1
Raccoons:
Friendly Bandits
Dr. Richard NeSmith

Issue 2
Sandhill Cranes
&
Pileated Woodpeckers
Flaming Redheads
Dr. Richard NeSmith

Issue 3
American
Alligators
&
Crocodiles
Dr. Richard NeSmith

Issue 4
Bobcats:
Ghostly Elusive
Dr. Richard NeSmith

Issue 5
Foxes:
Sneaky Rascals
Dr. Richard NeSmith

Issue 6
Armadillo:
Little Armored One
Dr. Richard NeSmith

Issue 7
Squirrels:
Bushy Tail Scampers
Dr. Richard NeSmith

Issue 8
River Otters:
Aquatic Clowns!
Dr. Richard NeSmith

Issue 9
Beavers:
Nature's Engineers !
Dr. Richard NeSmith

Issue 10
Black Bears
Titans of the Forest
Dr. Richard NeSmith

Issue 11
Freshwater
Turtles
Dr. Richard NeSmith

Issue 12
FUNGI, LICHENS
& MUSHROOMS
Dr. Richard NeSmith

Paperbacks: http://amazon.com/author/richardnesmith

e-books: https://bit.ly/3iuCgB3

---

[i] **Special thanks to the following who kindly provided permission to use their photographs.**

From Pixabay: Pezibear, Ronny Overhate, esudroff, Егор Камелев, Åsa Lundqvist, Adina Voicu, Hans Braxmeier, Heiko Stein, jplenio, and RitaE.

Finally, *special thanks* to likeminded friends who love wildlife and who willingly shared their wonderful photos, and many of whom have become my friends: **Anne Barca, Tom Dotson, Jackie Dibert, Stacey Diamond, Cindy Frasier, Greg Jowers, Tracie Minor, David Peters, Catherine Mishou Reese, Dr. Dan Rieck, Randy Johnson, Dr. Laurie Aleixo,** *and* **Dr. Michael Riffle**. *Special thanks* to Stacey Diamond for her *ideation* and *chimera* producing a snappy sub-title.

http://annebarcadesigns.com

JOHNSON ARTWORKS
http://johnsonartworks.com/)

If you enjoyed this book, please go to amazon.com and share a nice review. ☺

Thank you everyone.

Love Learning – Love Nature – Love Life

www.ingramcontent.com/pod-product-compliance
Lightning Source LLC
Chambersburg PA
CBHW040234240726
48664CB00001B/124